Into Literature

A BRIDGING COURSE TO ADVANCED STUDY

Sue Hackman and Barbara Marshall

Hodder & Stoughton

A MEMBER OF THE HODDER HEADLINE GROUP

British Library Cataloguing in Publication Data

1004631350

Hackman, Sue
    Into Literature: A Bridging Course to Advanced Study
    I. Title   II. Marshall, Barbara
    820.7

ISBN 0 340 64769 8

First published 1995
Impression number 10 9 8 7 6 5 4 3 2 1
Year   1999 1998 1997 1996 1995

Typeset by Litho Link Ltd, Welshpool, Powys, Wales.
Printed in Great Britain for Hodder & Stoughton Educational, a division of Hodder Headline Plc,
338 Euston Road, London NWI 3BH by Bath Press Ltd, Bath, Avon

Into
Literature

A BRIDGING COURSE TO ADVANCED STUDY

Acknowledgements

The authors would like to thank the students and staff at The Varndean College, Brighton.

The authors and publishers would like to thank the following for their kind permission to reproduce copyright material:

Anvil Press Poetry Ltd for 'Dream of a Lost Friend' from *The Other Country* by Carol Ann Duffy, published in 1990; Faber and Faber Ltd for 'The Waste Land' from *Collected Poems 1909–1962* by T S Eliot; Reed Consumer Books Ltd for 'Wee Horrors' from *Not, Not While the Giro* by James Kelman, first published by Martin Secker & Warburg Ltd; Transworld Publishers Ltd for 'Oh God Spare Youth' from *Let Me Make Myself Plain* by Catherine Cookson © 1988 Bantam Press. All rights reserved; A P Watt Ltd (Literary Agents) for 'Chemistry' from *Learning to Swim* by Graham Swift, first published by Picador in 1985.

Every effort has been made to trace and acknowledge ownership of copyright. The publisher will be glad to make suitable arrangements with any copyright holders whom they have been unable to contact.

Photographic acknowledgements

The publishers would like to thank the following for their kind permission to reproduce photographs in this book:

Timeline – British Museum (hieroglyphics); British Library (Beowulf, Canterbury Tales, Tyndale's Bible, Johnson's Dictionary); Mary Evans Picture Library (Bayeux Tapestry, Elizabeth I, Shakespeare, Great Fire of London, Queen Victoria, Karl Marx, suffragettes); Peter Newark's Pictures (printing press); Bodleian Library (Henry VIII); Bridgeman Art Library (Civil War, chimney sweeps); Fotomas Index (private subscription library); Penguin Books (*Ariel* paperback cover); Science & Society Picture Library (early colour TV).
Topham Picturepoint (p.14); Chris Davies (p.15); Sue Limb (p.23); The Wordsworth Trust (p.24); Adam Woolfitt/Robert Harding Picture Library (p.31); Nottinghamshire County Council Leisure Services (p.37); British Library (pp.48, 49); The Wordsworth Trust (p.49).

Introduction

This book is intended to open out your knowledge and understanding of literature, and to challenge you to find new meanings in texts. There are no perfectly correct answers to the questions we ask about literature. You will discover that there are as many meanings in literature as there are readers of it, and that the meanings can raise issues so contentious that they rock public opinion.

You can use this book in many ways to challenge and extend your thinking about literature, but one of its main intentions is to provide lessons for students who are about to embark on further study of literature. Other students who have a special interest in literature and wish to be challenged will also find this book useful.

Units One to Four of the book place literature in its social and cultural context. This provides an antidote to the close study of set texts required by examinations. If you study texts in detail for examination, you will learn a great deal about the imaginary world created in the text, but not necessarily about the real world in which the texts were written and read. Here is an opportunity to locate texts against their historical background and to consider how and why the texts we value today have been identified and chosen from all the other books written. You are about to devote hundreds of hours to the study of literature, and it is therefore worth asking the question, 'What *is* literature?'

Units Five to Seven explore the way texts are constructed. Texts challenge us to think, feel, empathise, imagine, predict, respond and sometimes to change ourselves, and the craft of the writer is to create the framework for this imaginative adventure. Unit Five investigates the narrative voice through which stories are filtered, and how this plays upon the reader. Unit Six considers the significance of form in making meaning, by contrasting a single event presented as a poem and as prose. Unit Seven studies the evolution of a poem through the stages of drafting, and considers the factors which inspire and constrain the writer.

Unit Eight is closer to home, but is very important. It explains in detail how you might progress from a first reading of a text to the final presentation of your ideas in essay form. The unit is based on a single, complete short story, but the approach can be adapted to other kinds of text. We hope that by the end of the unit you will feel more confident about your ability to perform well as a reader, as a student, and as a writer about literature.

All the activities in this book have been trialled in real classrooms. We have found that they can be made to work in many ways, but best of all through small-group discussion and debate. We thought long and hard about the order of the units, and finally decided on the one presented here, but each unit can be used independently, and you might prefer to start with Units Five, Six and Seven if you wish to work on personal interpretation first.

We estimate that each unit requires 2½ hours of work, but the material can be tailored to fit different timescales. The extension activities suggest ways of developing the units, and therefore require more time.

We hope that this book heightens your interest in literature and suggests some important questions for you to ask of the texts you study – but most of all we wish you great pleasure in your reading.

Contents

UNIT 1

TEXTS IN TIME AND PLACE

AIMS

- to give you a sense of how literature has developed over time
- to locate your set texts and authors in history
- to encourage you to research literature

ACTIVITY

- Open out the timeline (inside back cover) and read the poems A–F on pages 2–3. Think carefully about the style and content of the poems and then decide where to place them on the timeline, taking account of the historical information provided.

- Now read the prose extracts G–L on pages 4–5 and repeat the activity.

- Discuss the clues which helped you to date the extracts. Why were some texts more difficult to place than others?

- Now turn to page 8 where you will find information about the poems and prose.

- Research the birthplaces of the writers you have used in this unit and place them on the map.

Where to look

- A guide to English Literature, for example *The Oxford Companion to English Literature*. The reference section of your library should have guides similar to this.
- General encyclopaedias such as *Britannica* contain information about writers.
- The Literature and History sections of your library.
- The introductory notes to your set texts.
- Consult the Librarian about information on CD-ROM.

London

I wander through each chartered street,
Near where the chartered Thames does flow,
And mark in every face I meet
Marks of weakness, marks of woe.

In every cry of every man,
In every infant's cry of fear,
In every voice, in every ban,
The mind-forged manacles I hear.

How the chimney-sweeper's cry
Every blackening church appalls;
And the hapless soldier's sigh
Runs in blood down palace walls.

But most through midnight streets I hear
How the youthful harlot's curse
Blasts the newborn infant's tear,
And blights with plagues the marriage hearse.

One day I wrote her name upon the strand.
But came the waves and washèd it away:
Again I wrote it with a second hand
But came the tide, and made my pains his prey.
'Vain man,' said she, 'though do'st in vain assay.
A mortal thing so to immortalize.
For I myself shall like to this decay,
And eek my name be wipèd out likewise.
'Not so,' quoth I, 'let baser things devise
To die in dust, but you shall live by fame:
My verse your virtues rare shall eternize
And in the heavens write your glorious name.
Where, whenas death shall all the world subdue,
Our love shall live, and later life renew.

What Would I Give?

What would I give for a heart of flesh to warm me through,
Instead of this heart of stone ice-cold whatever I do;
Hard and cold and small, of all hearts the worst of all.

What would I give for words, if only words would come;
But now in its misery my spirit has fallen dumb:
Oh, merry friends, go your way, I have never a word to say.

What would I give for tears, not smiles but scalding tears,
To wash the black mark clean, and to thaw the frost of years,
To wash the stain ingrain and to make me clean again.

I sing of a maiden
That is makeles:
King of alle kinges
To here sone she ches.

He cam also stille
Ther his moder was,
As dew in Aprille
That falleth on the grass.

He cam also stille
To his moderes bowr,
As dew in Aprille
That falleth on the flowr.

He cam also stille
There his moder lay,
As dew in Aprille
That falleth on the spray.

Moder and maiden
Was never non but she:
Well may swich a lady
Godes moder be.

'Trams and dusty trees.
Highbury bore me. Richmond and Kew
Undid me. By Richmond I raised my knees
Supine on the floor of a narrow canoe.'

'My feet are at Moorgate, and my heart
Under my feet. After the event
He wept. He promised "a new start".
I made no comment. What should I resent?'

'On Margate Sands.
I can connect
Nothing with nothing.
The broken fingernails of dirty hands.
My people humble people who expect
Nothing.'
              la la

To Carthage then I came

Burning burning burning burning
O Lord Thou pluckest me out
O Lord Thou pluckest

burning

Upon a Girl of Seven Years Old

Wit's queen (if what the poets sing be true)
And Beauty's goddess, childhood never knew –
Pallas, they say, sprung from the head of Jove
Full grown, and from the sea the queen of Love;
But had they, Miss, your wit and beauty seen,
Venus and Pallas both had children been.
They, from the sweetness of that radiant look,
A copy of young Venus might have took,
And from those pretty things you speak have told
How Pallas talked when she was seven years old.

Fog everywhere. Fog up the river, where it flows among green aits and meadows; fog down the river, where it rolls defiled among the tiers of shipping, and the waterside pollutions of a great (and dirty) city. Fog on the Essex Marshes, fog on the Kentish heights. Fog creeping into the cabooses of collier-brigs; fog lying out on the yards, and hovering in the rigging of great ships; fog drooping on the gunwales of barges and small boats. Fog in the eyes and throats of ancient Greenwich pensioners, wheezing by the firesides of their wards; fog in the stem and bowl of the afternoon pipe of the wrathful skipper, down in his close cabin; fog cruelly pinching the toes and fingers of his shivering little 'prentice boy on deck. Chance people on the bridges peeping over the parapets into a nether sky of fog, with fog all round them, as if they were up in a balloon, and hanging in the misty clouds.

riverrun, past Eve and Adam's, from swerve of shore to bend of bay, brings us by a commodius vicus of recirculation back to Howth Castle and Environs.

Sir Tristram, violer d'amores, fr'over the short sea, had passencore rearrived from North Armorica on this side the scraggy isthmus of Europe Minor to wielderfight his penisolate war: nor had topsawyer's rocks by the stream Oconee exaggerated themselse to Laurens County's gorgios while they went doublin their mumper all the time: nor avoice from afire bellowsed mishe mishe to tauftauf thuartpeatrick: not yet, though venissoon after, had a kidscad buttended a bland old isaac: not yet, though all's fair in vanessy, were sosie sesthers wroth with twone nathandjoe. Rot a peck of pa's malt had Jhem or Shen brewed by arclight and rory end to the regginbrow was to be seen ringsome on the aquaface.

But what have I done with my life? thought Mrs. Ramsay, taking her place at the head of the table, and looking at all the plates making white circles on it. "William, sit by me," she said. "Lily," she said, wearily, "over there." They had that – Paul Rayley and Minta Doyle – she, only this – an infinitely long table and plates and knives. At the far end, was her husband, sitting down, all in a heap, frowning. What at? She did not know. She did not mind. She could not understand how she had ever felt any emotion or any affection for him. She had a sense of being past everything, through everything, out of everything, as she helped the soup, as if there was an eddy – there – and one could be in it, or one could be out of it, and she was out of it. It's all come to an end, she thought, while they came in one after another, Charles Tansley – "Sit there, please," she said – Augustus Carmichael – and sat down. And meanwhile she waited, passively, for someone to answer her, for something to happen. But this is not a thing, she thought, ladling out soup, that one says.

Being the third son of the family and not bred to any trade, my head began to be filled very early with rambling thoughts. My father, who was very ancient, had given me a competent share of learning, as far as house-education and a country free-school generally goes, and designed me for the law; but I would be satisfied with nothing but going to sea, and my inclination to this led me so strongly against the will, nay, the commands of my father, and against all the entreaties and perswasions of my mother and other friends, that there seemed to be something fatal in that propension of nature tending directly to the life of misery which was to befal me.

SIR WALTER ELLIOT, of Kellynch-hall, in Somersetshire, was a man who, for his own amusement, never took up any book but the Baronetage; there he found occupation for an idle hour, and consolation in a distressed one; there his faculties were roused into admiration and respect, by contemplating the limited remnant of the earliest patents; there any unwelcome sensations, arising from domestic affairs, changed naturally into pity and contempt, as he turned over the almost endless creations of the last century – and there, if every other leaf were powerless, he could read his own history with an interest which never failed – this was the page at which the favourite volume always opened:

ELLIOT OF KELLYNCH-HALL.

This time, I remembered I was lying in the oak closet, and I heard distinctly the gusty wind, and the driving of the snow; I heard, also, the fir-bough repeat its teasing sound, and ascribed it to the right cause; but it annoyed me so much, that I resolved to silence it, if possible; and, I thought, I rose and endeavoured to unhasp the casement. The hook was soldered into the staple, a circumstance observed by me when awake, but forgotten.

'I must stop it, nevertheless!' I muttered, knocking my knuckles through the glass, and stretching an arm out to seize the importunate branch: instead of which, my fingers closed on the fingers of a little, ice-cold hand!

The intense horror of nightmare came over me; I tried to draw back my arm, but the hand clung to it, and a most melancholy voice sobbed,

'Let me in – let me in!'

'Who are you?' I asked, struggling, meanwhile, to disengage myself.

- Do you notice any patterns in the distribution of writers on the timeline and the map? Consider:
  - time
  - place
  - type of text (e.g. poetry, drama, novel, non-fiction, short story)
  - gender of writer

Do there seem to be clusters or gaps? Can you account for them by referring to historical developments?

EXTENSION ACTIVITY_____

This activity involves making a wall display to show when and where key writers were working.

Make a large timeline and note on it the dates of well-known writers, famous works and your own set texts. Include historical information which you think is significant, such as important political events, periods of rapid social change, economic crisis and inventions. These need not be well-known events: for example the price of paper might be more useful than the name of the reigning monarch in giving us an idea about how texts were produced and who was able to buy them.

Increase the size of the map of Britain on page 6 or borrow a large one. Write the names and dates of British writers you have encountered on small tabs of paper, and use Blu-Tack to stick them on to the map in the correct location.

Increase the size of the world map below or borrow a large one. Repeat the activity above with the names and dates of world writers you have encountered.

The extracts selected for this timeline represent a tradition of highly regarded writers: the majority of lesser-known and unpublished writers have not been included. The writers also represent a very European culture, although literature from all over the world is being given increased recognition by the literary and educational establishment. The historical information we have been able to supply here is also very selective: the relationship between texts, their audience and the time they were produced can be very complex and interesting to research.

INFORMATION ABOUT TEXTS USED

Poetry

A   A poem by William Blake (1757–1827). Blake was writing at a time of political, industrial and agricultural revolution in Europe. The poem reflects his observations of great social change.

B   A sonnet by Edmund Spenser (1552–99). The sonnet, with its conventions of 14 lines, rhyme schemes, and metrical pattern of ten syllables per line, was very fashionable at the time. Poets continue to use it, particularly for 'emotional' poems.

C   A poem by Christina Rossetti (1830–94). Until this century there have been few well-known women poets.

D   An anonymous lyric of the early 1400s.

E   An extract from *The Wasteland* by T.S. Eliot (1888–1965). The style of the poem was a shock to its first readers.

F   A poem by Alexander Pope (1688–1744). It was fashionable to refer to myths and characters of the classical world.

Prose

G   The opening of *Bleak House* by Charles Dickens, published in monthly parts during 1852–3.

H   The opening of *Finnegan's Wake* by James Joyce, published in 1939.

I   An extract from *To The Lighthouse* by Virginia Woolf, published in 1927.

J   An extract from *Robinson Crusoe* by Daniel Defoe, published in 1719. Inspired by a true event, this was the first really successful novel.

K   The opening of *Persuasion* by Jane Austen, written in 1815–16 and published posthumously in 1818 (she died in 1817).

L   An extract from *Wuthering Heights* by Emily Bronte 1847, first published under the pseudonym, Ellis Bell.

2

WHAT IS LITERATURE?

AIMS

- ■ to raise issues about reading and evaluating texts
- ■ to raise awareness about how and why some texts become regarded as part of the canon of 'great literature'
- ■ to reflect on the significance of personal preference

ACTIVITY

The editors of a forthcoming anthology entitled *Great English Verse* have asked you to select four poems to go in a section on 'Death'.

- • Make a list of the criteria you think you should consider when evaluating the poems.

The contending poems are listed below. Read them carefully before you discuss your selection, paying particular attention to the factors which influence your decisions.

A

'Even such is time'

Even such is time, which takes in trust
Our youth, our joys, and all we have,
And pays us but with age and dust:
Who in the dark and silent grave
When we have wandered all our ways
Shuts up the story of our days.
And from which earth and grave and dust
The Lord shall raise me up, I trust.

B

The Dead

These hearts were woven of human joys and cares,
Washed marvellously with sorrow, swift to mirth.
The years had given them kindness. Dawn was theirs,
And sunset, and the colours of the earth.
These had seen movement, and heard music; known
Slumber and waking; loved; gone proudly friended;
Felt the quick stir of wonder; sat alone;
Touched flowers and furs and cheeks. All this is ended.

There are waters blown by changing winds to laughter
And lit by the rich skies, all day. And after,
Frost, with a gesture, stays the waves that dance
And wandering loveliness. He leaves a white
Unbroken glory, a gathered radiance,
A width, a shining peace, under the night.

C

Song

When I am dead, my dearest,
Sing no sad songs for me;
Plant thou no roses at my head,
Nor shady cypress tree:
Be the green grass above me
With showers and dewdrops wet;
And if thou wilt, remember,
And if thou wilt, forget.

I shall not see the shadows,
I shall not feel the rain;
I shall not hear the nightingale
Sing on, as if in pain;
And dreaming through the twilight
That doth not rise nor set,
Haply I may remember,
And haply may forget.

D

Nothing is more precious
Than the thoughts we have of you,
To us you were so special
God must have thought so too.

E

Dream of a Lost Friend

You were dead, but we met, dreaming,
before you had died. Your name, twice,
then you turned, pale, unwell. *My dear,
my dear, must this be?* A public building
where I've never been, and, on the wall,
an AIDS poster. Your white lips. *Help me.*

We embraced, standing in a long corridor
which harboured a fierce pain neither of us felt yet.
The words you spoke were frenzied prayers
to Chemistry; or you laughed, a child-man's laugh,
innocent, hysterical, out of your skull. *It's only
a dream,* I heard myself saying, *only a bad dream.*

Some of our best friends nurture a virus, an idle,
charmed, purposeful enemy, and it dreams
they are dead already. In fashionable restaurants,
over the crudités, the healthy imagine a time
when all these careful moments will be dreamed
and dreamed again. *You look well. How do you feel?*

Then, as I slept, you backed away from me, crying
and offering a series of dates for lunch, waving.
I missed your funeral, I said, knowing you couldn't hear
at the end of the corridor, thumbs up, acting.
Where there's life . . . Awake, alive, for months I think of you
almost hopeful in a bad dream where you were long dead.

F

Oh God spare youth
To see this life,
To experience the love, the joy
The anguish, the wonder, the strife;
Don't deprive them of summer
While in their spring,
Give them the chance
To let their minds soar,
To let their hands clutch the mountain tops,
Their bodies to dive deep from the rock;
Don't cut short their time
On the ancient clock of destiny;
Keep from their marrow
Disease that is due to age;
Don't take their breath
While yet they fear death;
Give them a span in which to know courage
Is the friend of pain;
Give them the time to live, be a wife
And create themselves again;
But if You must take them,
Do it before they smell
The scent of life.

G

Fragment on Death

And Paris be it or Helen dying,
Who dies soever, dies with pain.
He that lacks breath and wind for sighing,
His gall bursts on his heart; and then
He sweats, God knows what sweat! again,
No man may ease him of his grief;
Child, brother, sister, none were fain
To bail him thence for his relief.

Death makes him shudder, swoon, wax pale,
Nose bend, veins stretch, and breath surrender,
Neck swell, flesh soften, joints that fail
Crack their strained nerves and arteries slender.
O woman's body found so tender,
Smooth, sweet, so precious in men's eyes,
Must thou too bear such count to render?
Yes; or pass quick into the skies.

For the Fallen

With proud thanksgiving, a mother for her children,
England mourns for her dead across the sea.
Flesh of her flesh they were, spirit of her spirit,
Fallen in the cause of the free.

Solemn the drums thrill: Death august and royal
Sings sorrow up into immortal spheres.
There is music in the midst of desolation
And a glory that shines upon our tears.

They went with songs to the battle, they were young,
Straight of limb, true of eye, steady and aglow.
They were staunch to the end against odds uncounted,
They fell with their faces to the foe.

They shall grow not old, as we that are left grow old:
Age shall not weary them, nor the years condemn.
At the going down of the sun and in the morning
We will remember them.

They mingle not with their laughing comrades again;
They sit no more at familiar tables of home;
They have no lot in our labour of the day-time:
They sleep beyond England's foam.

But where our desires are and our hopes profound,
Felt as a well-spring that is hidden from sight,
To the innermost heart of their own land they are known
As the stars are known to the Night.

As the stars that shall be bright when we are dust,
Moving in marches upon the heavenly plain,
As the stars that are starry in the time of our darkness,
To the end, to the end, they remain.

On My First Son

Farewell, thou child of my right hand, and joy;
My sin was too much hope of thee, loved boy.
Seven years thou wert lent to me, and I thee pay,
Exacted by thy fate, on the just day.
Oh, could I lose all father now! For why
Will man lament the state he should envy?
To have so soon 'scaped world's and flesh's rage,
And, if no other misery, yet age?
Rest in soft peace, and, asked, say here doth lie
Ben Jonson his best piece of poetry;
For whose sake, henceforth, all his vows be such,
As what he loves may never like too much.

- Compare selections and discuss the factors which influenced your decisions. How far did you agree on a list of criteria for selecting poems for an anthology such as this?

- If you made a different selection, based on personal preference, how would it compare to the choice made for the anthology? Can you account for this?

- Now look at the information provided on page 17. Would you revise your selection in the light of this new information? Why?

All published books pass through a selection procedure and even then not all of them are successful in the market. Books do not have to be best sellers to be highly regarded.

- Who decides which books are quality literature? For example, how do the following influence this process?

  - Publishers
  - Readers – members of the public
  - Reviewers/critics in newspapers or on television
  - Academics
  - The government
  - Teachers
  - Competition judges
  - Writers

EXTENSION ACTIVITY_____

Spend some time finding two poems on the theme of love. If there is class time available, hold an editorial meeting to select a class anthology of love poems to represent a choice from each member of the group. Each entry chosen must be accompanied by a short commentary justifying its inclusion.

Preferences vary among individuals and over time. Texts which are valued by one generation fall out of favour with another, as the cultural climate changes. In the age of mass publication, what is popular is not always the same as what is regarded as quality literature. The definition of 'Literature' has been challenged by the development of cheap paperbacks, film, television and other forms of mass media.

INFORMATION ABOUT THE TEXTS USED

A   *Even such is time* by Sir Walter Raleigh (1554–1618)
The famous Elizabethan explorer was executed for treason. This poem was found in his prison at the Tower of London after his execution.

B   *The Dead* by Rupert Brooke (1887–1915)
Brooke died in the First World War. Although he was extremely popular with readers for some decades after the war, his work does not have the academic respect of the other famous war poets such as Wilfred Owen.

C   *Song* by Christina Rossetti (1830–94)
Christina is probably less well known than her brothers, the artists and writers who set up the Pre-Raphaelite Brotherhood in the 1840s. This group was particularly interested in being truthful to nature and in moral and religious issues. This poem however, is a popular one, featured in *The Collins Book of Best-loved Verse.*

D   *Nothing is more precious*
An epitaph from a tombstone.

E   *Dream of a Lost Friend* by Carol Ann Duffy
This poem is from *The Other Country,* published in 1990. Duffy is a highly regarded contemporary poet who often features on advanced level syllabuses.

F   *Oh God Spare Youth* by Catherine Cookson
This is from an anthology of Catherine Cookson's writing. A popular novelist, she is hesitant to describe herself as a poet and calls her work 'Prose On Short Lines'.

G   *Fragment on Death* by Algernon Charles Swinburne (1837–1909)
Swinburne was a Victorian poet associated with the Pre-Raphaelites and considered to be immoral in his verse and lifestyle. Like many of the Victorian poets well known in their time, his work became unfashionable in the early twentieth century.

H   *For the Fallen* by R. L. Binyon
This poem is recited as a mark of respect to the dead of two world wars at annual remembrance services all over Britain on Armistice Day.

I   *On My First Son* by Ben Jonson (c.1573–1637)
Ben Jonson was a poet and dramatist, and was famous as Shakespeare's rival. This poem was written about his son (also Benjamin Jonson) who died of the plague in 1603.

3

TEXT AND CONTEXT

AIMS

- ■ to illustrate the range of influences and constraints which have an effect on the writing of Literature
- ■ to demonstrate how a knowledge of the context in which a text was written can inform the reader's interpretation of it
- ■ to recognise that texts are written and read in an historical context

ACTIVITY

This activity is staged in four parts.

I The poem

- • Read the following poem and discuss what you understand about it. Share your reactions and impressions.

Beggars

She had a tall man's height or more;
Her face from summer's noontide heat
No bonnet shaded, but she wore
A mantle, to her very feet
Descending with a graceful flow,
And on her head a cap as white as newfallen snow.

Her skin was of Egyptian brown:
Haughty, as if her eyes had seen
Its own light to a distance thrown,
She towered, fit person for a Queen
To lead those ancient Amazonian files;
Or ruling Bandit's wife among the Grecian isles.

Advancing, forth she stretched her hand
And begged an alms with doleful plea
That ceased not; on our English land
Such woes, I knew, could never be;
And yet a boon I gave her, for the creature
Was beautiful to see – a weed of glorious feature.

I left her, and pursued my way;
And soon before me did espy
A pair of little Boys at play,
Chasing a crimson butterfly;
The taller followed with his hat in hand,
Wreathed round with yellow flowers the gayest of the land.

The other wore a rimless crown
With leaves of laurel stuck about;
And, while both followed up and down,
Each whooping with a merry shout,
In their fraternal features I could trace
Unquestionable lines of that wild Suppliant's face.

Yet *they*, so blithe of heart, seemed fit
For finest tasks of earth or air:
Wings let them have, and they might flit
Precursors to Aurora's car,
Scattering fresh flowers; though happier far, I ween,
To hunt their fluttering game o'er rock and level green.

They dart across my path – but lo,
Each ready with a plaintive whine!
Said I, 'not half an hour ago
Your Mother has had alms of mine.'
'That cannot be,' one answered – 'she is dead:'
I looked reproof – they saw – but neither hung his head.

'She has been dead, Sir, many a day.' –
'Hush, boys! you're telling me a lie;
It was your Mother, as I say!'
And, in the twinkling of an eye,
'Come! Come!' cried one, and without more ado,
Off to some other play the joyous Vagrants flew!

- When do you think the poem was written and what kind of society does it describe? What is the poet's attitude to the female beggar and beggary in general?

2 About beggary

The poem was written in 1802 when the industrial and agricultural revolutions were creating a new underclass of desperately poor people. Beggary was widespread and there was no system of social security. Food was often expensive. The very poor depended on begging to survive. Every community had local beggars, but there were also more travellers moving around the country in search of work and charity. Beggary was part of everyday life. It was considered acceptable and even natural that some people should be sunk so low. The poet was unusual in portraying the beggar as having dignity.

- Discuss together your own encounters with beggars and your reactions to this subject.

- What difficulties might you experience in trying to write a similar poem today? Would it be acceptable?

- Bearing in mind the social changes which have occurred, do you think a modern reader has a different reaction from one at the time the poem *Beggars* was first published?

3 The origin of the poem

The poem was written by William Wordsworth in 1802. Wordsworth was living in the English Lake District at this time, sharing a house with his sister Dorothy. Today he is regarded as one of the most important poets in English literature. The poem was not written from first-hand experience. It is, however, based on a true incident. It happened to Dorothy two years before the poem was written. Dorothy wrote about it in her journal, which William often used as a source for his poems.

On Tuesday, May 27th, a very tall woman, tall much beyond the measure of tall women, called at the door. She had on a very long brown cloak, and a very white cap, without bonnet; her face was excessively brown, but it had plainly once been fair. She led a little bare-footed child about 2 years old by the hand, and said her husband, who was a tinker, was gone before with the other children. I gave her a piece of bread. Afterwards on my road to Ambleside, beside the bridge at Rydale, I saw her husband sitting by the roadside, his two asses feeding beside him, and the two young children at play upon the grass. The man did not beg. I passed on and about ¼ mile further I saw two boys before me, one about 10, the other about 8 years old, at play chasing a butterfly. They were wild figures not very ragged, but without shoes and stockings; the hat of the elder was wreathed round with yellow flowers, the younger whose hat was only a rimless crown, had stuck it round with laurel leaves. They continued to play till I drew very near, and then they addressed me with the begging cant and the whining voice of sorrow. I said 'I served your mother this morning'. (The Boys were so like the woman who had called at the door that I could not be mistaken.) 'O!' says the elder, 'you could not serve my mother for she's dead, and my father's on at the next town – he's a potter.' I persisted in my assertion, and that I would give them nothing. Says the elder, 'Come, let's away', and away they flew like lightning. They had however sauntered so long in their road that they did not reach Ambleside before me, and I saw them go up to Matthew Harrison's house with their wallet upon the elder's shoulder, and creeping with a beggar's complaining foot. On my return through Ambleside I met in the street the mother driving her asses; in the two panniers of one of which were the two little children, whom she was chiding and threatening with a wand she used to drive her asses, while the little things hung in wantonness over the pannier's edge. The woman had told me in the morning that she was from Scotland, which her accent fully proved, but that she had lived (I think) at Wigton, that they could not keep a house and so they travelled.

Wordsworth used Dorothy's journals as the starting-point for his poems on many occasions. The famous poems called *The Daffodils*, *The Butterfly*, and *The Leech-gatherer* were all culled from her notebook.

- How far has William drawn on Dorothy's writing?

- Is it reasonable for one writer to borrow from another in this way?

4 Dorothy and William

Until recently Dorothy's poems and journals were neglected and her work has never received the recognition afforded to William. Colette Clark, the editor of her journals, wrote in 1960: 'Dorothy Wordsworth was one of those sweet characters whose only life lies in their complete dedication to a man of genius'.

Dorothy did aspire to being a poet in her own right, as this unpublished poem demonstrates.

Extract from *Irregular verses*

You ask why in that jocund time
Why did I not in jingling rhyme
Display those pleasant guileless dreams
That furnished still exhaustless themes?
– I *reverenced* the Poet's skill,
And *might have* nursed a mounting Will
To imitate the tender Lays
Of them who sang in Nature's praise;
But bashfulness, a struggling shame
A fear that elder heads might blame
– Or something worse – a lurking pride
Whispering my playmates would deride
Stifled ambition, checked the aim
If e'er by chance 'the numbers came'
– Nay even the mild maternal smile,
That oft-times would repress, beguile
The over-confidence of youth,
Even that dear smile, to own the truth,
Was dreaded by a fond self-love;
''Twill glance on me – and to reprove
Or,' (sorest wrong in childhood's school)
'Will *point* the sting of ridicule.'

- From your reading of this poem what do you think discouraged Dorothy from pursuing her ambition to become a well-known writer?

- Can you think of other reasons why there are so few women poets before this century?

Dorothy settled instead to serving William. She shared with him her own writings and made neat copies of his poems.

We see Wordsworth as a great poet, but he saw himself as a social critic: 'Although he was known to the world only as a poet he had given twelve hours' thought to the conditions and prospects of society for one to poetry.'

His political views were radical and left-wing: he was very influenced by the ideals of the French Revolution such as democracy, freedom and equality. He was writing poetry which challenged tradition in quite daring ways: its language was plainer, its subject matter was ordinary people and the ballad form he used was quite unlike the grand and learned poetry that was fashionable at the time.

In later life, Wordsworth changed his political views, and became rather conservative and preoccupied with himself.

EXTENSION ACTIVITY

Wordsworth belonged to a group of writers who have since been labelled as 'Romantic' poets, although this was not a term they applied to themselves. Read some of the poems of Blake, Coleridge, Shelley, Keats or Byron. Research what is meant by the term 'Romantic'.

Over the centuries an image of Wordsworth has evolved as a poet of the emotions who worshipped all things natural. The Lake District has become a tourist shrine to Wordsworth. Like the other Romantic poets, his political commitments are given less attention. He has been 'packaged'.

4

USING THE IMAGINATION

AIMS

- to demonstrate the role of the reader in making sense of the text
- to underline the importance of previous experience in reading
- to encourage reflective reading

ACTIVITY

- Read this passage which is the opening of Ian McEwan's novel *The Cement Garden*. As you read, notice what thoughts, feelings, images and ideas pass through your mind. Jot down these reflections privately on a piece of paper.

I did not kill my father, but I sometimes felt I had helped him on his way. And but for the fact that it coincided with a landmark in my own physical growth, his death seemed insignificant compared with what followed. My sisters and I talked about him the week after he died, and Sue certainly cried when the ambulance men tucked him up in a bright-red blanket and carried him away. He was a frail, irascible, obsessive man with yellowish hands and face. I am only including the little story of his death to explain how my sisters and I came to have such a large quantity of cement at our disposal.

In the early summer of my fourteenth year a lorry pulled up outside our house. I was sitting on the front step rereading a comic. The driver and another man came towards me. They were covered in a fine, pale dust which gave their faces a ghostly look.

They were both whistling shrilly completely different tunes. I stood up and held the comic out of sight. I wished I had been reading the racing page of my father's paper, or the football results.

'Cement?' one of them said. I hooked my thumbs into my pockets, moved my weight on to one foot and narrowed my eyes a little. I wanted to say something terse and appropriate, but I was not sure I had heard them right. I left it too long, for the one who had spoken rolled his eyes towards the sky and with his hands on his hips stared past me at the front door. It opened and my father stepped out biting his pipe and holding a clipboard against his hip.

- What were you thinking and feeling as you read the passage? Did you:
  - see images in your mind's eye? What were they?
  - jump to conclusions about the narrator? Is it a male or a female? Age? Character?
  - ask yourself questions and remark on the passage? What things did you remark upon?
  - predict what was going to happen? In the short term? In the long term?
  - read some bits over again? Which bits and why?
  - change your mind about anything? What prompted the change?
  - take a like or dislike to the writing? What appealed or offended?
  - feel reminded of something else you had read? What reminded you of it?
  - relate your reading to your own experiences? In what ways?

- Share your findings in a group, and notice the similarities and dissimilarities in your responses. How do you account for them?

- How far is your reading influenced and supported by previous experience of life and literature?

- Consider these two-word extracts. What kind of texts do they come from and how do you know? (You can check your guesses at the end of the section.)

First, whisk

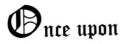

Hydrocarbons react

Today I

In conclusion

Hear, sweet

Find five different types of writing:
1   A set of instructions, such as a recipe or a repair manual
2   A piece of factual information, such as an entry in an encyclopaedia
3   A piece of reporting, such as a newspaper story or a magazine article
4   A piece of writing expressing an opinion, such as an editorial, a manifesto or a campaign leaflet
5   An advertisement, such as one in a colour supplement magazine

Each kind of writing has its own rules and conventions, and they are significantly different from narrative.
Either individually or in groups sharing materials, work out the conventions of each type of writing. Consider:

– the layout and appearance of the text
– the order in which the information is arranged
– the kind of vocabulary used
– the way the sentences are organised
– whether it is written in the present, past or future tense
– whether it is personal or impersonal

Is there any reason why these conventions have been chosen? Consider the likely readers and their purpose for reading.

Reading is a creative activity. The imagination is busy making sense of the text, not simply by getting involved but also by making judgements about it. One of the skills of reading literature at advanced level is to identify those aspects of the text which give rise to thoughts and feelings.

The more we read, the more familiar we become with the way different texts work. We look out for familiar patterns and begin to develop expectations and tastes. We become more skilful in using information.

'TWO-WORD EXTRACTS' ANSWERS

Letter
Recipe
Children's story
A piece of persuasive writing
Chemistry textbook
Diary
Poem

Letter

First, whisk

Recipe

Once upon

Children's story

Hydrocarbons react

Chemistry textbook

Today I

Diary

Hear, sweet

Poem

In conclusion

A piece of persuasive writing

5

THE NARRATIVE VOICE

AIMS

- to investigate the way writers create the voice of the narrator
- to examine assumptions about fiction and non-fiction
- to consider how texts unfold

ACTIVITY

This activity involves reading a complete short text in stages. Discuss one stage at a time. Do not move on until you have completed your discussion.

Stage 1

1

Wee horrors

The backcourt was thick with rubbish as usual. What a mess. I never like thinking about the state it used to get into. As soon as a family flitted out to the new home all the weans were in and dragging off the abandoned furnishings & fittings, most of which they dumped. Plus with the demolition work going on you were getting piles of mortar and old brickwork everywhere. A lot of folk thought the worst kind of rubbish was the soft goods, the mattresses and dirty clothing left behind by the ragmen. Fleas were the problem. It seemed like every night of the week we were having to root them out once the weans came in. Both breeds we were catching, the big yins and the wee yins, the dark and the rusty brown. The pest-control went round from door to door. Useless. The only answer was keeping the weans inside but ours were too old for that. Having visitors in the house was an ordeal, trying to listen to what they were saying while watching for the first signs of scratching.

- From your reading of the opening, what kind of person is the narrator? Discuss the evidence.

Stage 2

2

Then last thing at night, before getting into bed, me and the wife had to make a point of checking through our own stuff. Apart from that there was little to be done about it. We did warn the weans but it was useless. Turn your back and they were off downstairs to play at wee houses, dressing-up in the clothes and bouncing on the mattresses till all you were left hoping was they would knock the stuffing out the fleas. Some chance. You have to drown the cunts or burn them. A few people get the knack of crushing them between thumbnail and forefinger but I could never master that.

Anyway, fleas have got nothing to do with time. I was down in the backcourt to shout my pair up for their tea. The woman up the next close had told me they were all involved in some new den they had built and if I saw hers while I was at it I was to send them up right away. The weans were always making dens. It could be funny to see. You looked out the window and saw what you thought was a pile of rubble and maybe a sheet of tarpaulin stuck on the top. Take another look and you might see a wee head poking out, then another, and another, till finally maybe ten of them were standing there, thinking the coast was clear. But on this occasion I couldn't see a thing. I checked out most of the possibilities. Nothing. No signs of them anywhere. And it was quiet as well. Normally you would've at least heard a couple of squeaks. I tramped about for a time, retracing my steps and so on. I was not too worried. It would have been different if only my pair was missing but there was no sight nor sound of any description. And I was having to start considering the dunnies. This is where I got annoyed. I've always hated dunnies – pitchblack and that smell of charred rubbish, the broken glass, these things your shoes nudge against. Terrible. Then if you're in one and pause a moment there's this silence forcing you to listen. Really bad. I had to go down but. In the second one I tried I found some of the older mob, sitting in a kind of circle round two candles. They heard me come and I knew they had shifted something out of sight, but they recognised me okay and one of the lassies told me she had seen a couple of weans sneaking across to Greegor's. I was really angry at this. I had told them umpteen times never to go there. By rights the place should've got knocked down months ago but progress was being blocked for some reason I dont know, and now the squatters and a couple of the girls were in through the barricading. If you looked over late at night you could see the candle glow at the windows and during the day you were getting the cars crawling along near the pavement. It was hopeless. I went across. Once upon a time a grocer had a shop in the close and this had something to do with how it got called Greegor's. Judging from the smell of food he was still in business. At first I thought it was coming from up the close but the nearer I got I could tell it was coming from the dunny. Down I went. Being a corner block there were a good few twists and turns from the entrance lobby and I was having to go carefully. It felt like planks of wood I was walking on. Then the sounds. A kind of sizzling – making you think of a piece of fucking silverside in the oven, these crackling noises when the juice spurts out. Jesus christ. I shouted the names of my pair. The sound of feet scuffling. I turned a corner and got a hell of a shock – a woman standing in a doorway. Her face wasnt easy to see because of the light from behind her. Then a man appeared. He began nodding away with a daft smile on his face.

- What do you think will happen next?

Stage 3

─────────────────────── **3** ───────────────────────

I recognised them. Wineys. they had been dossing about the area for the past while. Even the face she had told a story, white with red blotches, eyes always seeming to water. She walked in this queer kind of stiff shuffle, her shoes flapping. When she stepped back from the doorway she drew the cuff of her coat sleeve across her mouth. The man was still giving his daft smiles. I followed. Inside the room all the weans were gathered round the middle of the floor. Sheets of newspaper had been spread about. I spotted my pair immediately – scared out their wits at seeing me. I just looked at them. Over at the fireplace a big fire was going, not actually in the fireplace, set to about a yard in front. The spit was fashioned above it and a wee boy stood there, he must've been rotating the fucking thing. Three lumps of meat sizzled away and just to the side were a few cooked bits lined in a row. I hadnt noticed the woman walk across but then she was there and making a show of turning the contraption just so I would know she wasnt giving a fuck about me being there. And him – still smiling, then beginning to make movements as if he wanted to demonstrate how it all worked. He was pointing out a row of raw lumps on the mantelpiece and then reaching for a knife with a thin blade.

- There are two sentences left. What are you expecting?

4

I shook my head, jesus christ right enough. I grabbed for my pair,
yelling at the rest of the weans to get up that effing stair at once.

- What do you think this story is about?

    - Split into two groups.
      Group 1 should use textual evidence to argue that this is a factual
      account.
      Group 2 should use textual evidence to argue that this is a work
      of fiction.
      You may find it useful to read aloud sections of the text to sample
      the voice of the narrator. Also, consider how far the narrator has
      manipulated your responses, for example through arousing your
      anticipation, use of imagery, and the way the story is presented
      and paced.

E X T E N S I O N   A C T I V I T Y_____

Produce two written pieces, each less than one side long.
One should be a true account of a personal experience and
the other a short piece of fiction. Members of your group
should then identify which is which.

What do you notice about the organisation and choice of
language in each case?

Is there a significant difference in composing from real
experience and imagined experience?

Fiction draws on real experience. Real events are presented in language.
Something is often changed, lost or added in the telling.

UNIT

6

PROSE AND POETRY

AIMS

- to illuminate the relationship between poetry and prose
- to draw attention to the importance of form in making meaning
- to identify techniques used by writers to create particular effects

ACTIVITY

Stage 1

- Make two columns headed 'Poetry' and 'Narrative fiction'. Under each heading write down all the features you think are distinctive about the way each is written. Include similarities as well as differences. You might consider, for example, aspects of the language, content, and form.

Stage 2

- Read the poem below and discuss what interests, puzzles or pleases you about it.

Discord in Childhood

Outside the house an ash-tree hung its terrible whips,
And at night when the wind rose, the lash of the tree
Shrieked and slashed the wind, as a ship's
Weird rigging in a storm shrieks hideously.

Within the house two voices arose, a slender lash
Whistling she-delirious rage, and the dreadful sound
Of a male thong booming and bruising, until it had drowned
The other voice in a silence of blood, 'neath the noise of the ash.

The poem was written by D. H. Lawrence and is said to be based on a personal experience. The same experience is described in his novel *Sons and Lovers*.

- Read the following passage from the novel.

When William was growing up, the family moved from the Bottoms to a house on the brow of the hill, commanding a view of the valley, which spread out like a convex cockle-shell, or a clamp-shell, before it. In front of the house was a huge old ash-tree. The west wind, sweeping from Derbyshire, caught the houses with full force, and the tree shrieked again. Morel liked it.

'It's music,' he said. 'It sends me to sleep.'

But Paul and Arthur and Annie hated it. To Paul it became almost a demoniacal noise. The winter of their first year in the new house their father was very bad. The children played in the street, on the brim of the wide, dark valley, until eight o'clock. Then they went to bed. Their mother sat sewing below. Having such a great space in front of the house gave the children a feeling of night, of vastness, and of terror. This terror came in from the shrieking of the tree and the anguish of the home discord. Often Paul would wake up, after he had been asleep a long time, aware of thuds downstairs. Instantly he was wide awake. Then he heard the booming shouts of his father, come home nearly drunk, then the sharp replies of his mother, then the bang, bang of his father's fist on the table, and the nasty snarling shout as the man's voice got higher. And then the whole was drowned in a piercing medley of shrieks and cries from the great, windswept ash-tree. The children lay silent in suspense, waiting for a lull in the wind to hear what their father was doing. He might hit their mother again. There was a feeling of horror, a kind of bristling in the darkness, and a sense of blood. They lay with their hearts in the grip of an intense anguish. The wind came through the tree fiercer and fiercer. All the cords of the great harp hummed, whistled, and shrieked. And then came the horror of the sudden silence, silence everywhere, outside and downstairs. What was it? Was it a silence of blood? What had he done?

The children lay and breathed the darkness. And then, at last, they heard their father throw down his boots and tramp upstairs in his stockinged feet. Still they listened. Then at last, if the wind allowed, they heard the water of the tap drumming into the kettle, which their mother was filling for morning, and they could go to sleep in peace.

So they were happy in the morning – happy, very happy
playing, dancing at night round the lonely lamp-post in the midst
of the darkness. But they had one tight place of anxiety in their
hearts, one darkness in their eyes, which showed all their lives.

Stage 3

- Compare the literary form of the two versions. Consider their shape and organisation, use of language and effect on the reader. It will be helpful if you read aloud both versions, listening for their special sounds and structures.

- Did the two pieces conform to the expectations of poetry and narrative you listed in stage 1?

- Can you find examples which illustrate each of the items in your Poetry/Narrative fiction columns?

EXTENSION ACTIVITY

Make a single list of all the ways in which writers manipulate words to create a particular effect, for example the use of rhythm or the use of alliteration (repeated initial sounds). Illustrate your list with examples from this activity.

Keep this list for future reference, and add to it during your course.

We bring certain expectations to both poetry and prose which are not always justified. It is interesting to reflect where these ideas come from and how our attitudes to literature are formed. Surveys have shown that poetry is particularly unpopular with boys. Historically poetry was considered highbrow, the pursuit of people from the leisured classes.

At advanced level, examiners often complain that students 'spot' techniques in writing without describing how these techniques work in the text. They also complain that students throw in literary terms without relating them to the ideas expressed. Terms are useful because they save cumbersome explanations, but only in the context of discussing the writer's meaning and your response to it.

7

THE WRITING PROCESS

AIMS

- to illuminate the processes of writing
- to explore the choices writers make
- to highlight factors which influence composition

ACTIVITY

In this activity you will be looking closely at the drafts of Carol Rumens' poem, *Moment of Faith*.

I was asked by Birthright, a charity researching into safer childbirth, to write a poem for an exhibition on the theme of Mother and Child. I decided to interpret the theme literally, because I have long felt I wanted to write more about the birth of my first child.

Carol Rumens

Here are six versions of Carol Rumens' poem, including five of her drafts and the 'final' poem. They are presented out of sequence.

- Read the poems closely in order to determine which is the finished version, then attempt to sequence them in the order they were written.

A

It was the crying hand
Thrust from the shawl, a sharp-petalled
Celandine in cold March grass:

It was the five little swimmers,
Sea-wearied, bent at the waist,
Still waxed in each wrinkle and seam:

It was the stronghold they closed
Round her probing finger, the way
The crying shivered into stillness,

That made her think that the teeming
Shambles of it all was planned,
And the plan was matchless.

B

It was the crying hand
that stuck out tense, fully opened
like the sudden appearance of a star

it was the way the palm
and each of the little jointed wands
was waxed for its own protection

that made her think
that this had somehow all been planned
and when she touched it

it was the way the hand folded
shut round her stroking finger
and the crying died away

that made her begin to dream
that somehow it had all been planned
and the plan was matchless.

C

It was the crying hand
Thrust from the shawl, unannounced
As celandines in March grass.

It was the five little swimmers,
Sea-wearied, bent at the waist,
Still waxed in each wrinkle and seam.

It was the stronghold they closed
Round her probing finger, the way
The crying shivered, and ceased,

That made her think that the teeming
Shambles of it all was planned,
And the plan was matchless.

D

It was the crying hand
Thrust from the shawl, wide-opened:
a celandine in cold March grass

It was the way the palm
And each little jointed wand
had been carefully waxed like a swimmer

It was the way it clammed
Tight round her probing finger
And the crying shivered into stillness

That made her begin to imagine
This had somehow all been planned
and the plan was matchless.

E

It was the crying hand
Thrust from the shawl, a sharp-petalled
Celandine in cold March grass:

It was the five little swimmers,
Sea-wearied, bent at the waist,
Waxed still in each hair-fine crease:

It was the sealed fortress
They built round her terrified finger
As the crying shivered into stillness

That made her think that the seeming
Shambles of it all was planned
And that the plan was matchless.

F

It was the crying hand
Thrust from the shawl, unannounced
Celandine in cold March grass:

It was the five little swimmers,
Waxed in each wrinkle and seam,
Bent at waist, sea-wearied.

It was the stronghold they closed
Round her probing finger, the way
The crying shivered into stillness.

That made her think that the teeming
Shambles of it all was planned,
And the plan was matchless.

41

- When you have completed this task, read Carol Rumens' own commentary on the process of writing the poem.

I was asked by Birthright, a charity researching into safer childbirth, to write a poem for an exhibition on the theme of Mother and Child. I decided to interpret the theme literally, because I have long felt I wanted to write more about the birth of my first child, and particularly the moment of 'bonding' which I remember extremely well. She had been washed and wrapped and put in my arms; she was crying lustily and one of her little hands stuck out of the shawl. I stroked the palm with my own finger and this tiny hand shut round it and the crying stopped! It was the most magical thing that had ever happened to me. I'd hardly ever *seen* a baby before, and didn't have a clue how to look after one. But at that moment I felt I was a mother.

I realised this would be a risky thing to write about, so never did. (My early birth-poems are dreadful, Plath-derivative, blood-and-guts stuff.) Having the commission decided me: I'd write that poem which has been waiting for twenty-one years! The first four drafts show its gestation from the time of the commission to the publication – about three months. I should add that, eventually, a sequence of ten birth poems sprang up around it. Some of these are still work-in-progress.

First draft:

```
It was the crying hand
that stuck out tense, fully opened
like the sudden appearance of a star

it was the way the palm
and each of the little jointed wands
was waxed for its own protection

that made her think
that this had somehow all been planned
and when she touched it

it was the way the hand folded
shut round her stroking finger
and the crying died away

that made her begin to dream
that somehow it had all been planned
and the plan was matchless.
```

When I got to the last stanza, I realised that this was where the material originally put in the third stanza should go, so my next step was to erase stanza three.

The next draft was typed:

```
It was the crying hand
Thrust from the shawl, wide-opened:
a celandine in cold March grass

It was the way the palm
And each little jointed wand
had been carefully waxed like a swimmer

It was the way it clammed
Tight round her probing finger
And the crying shivered into stillness

That made her begin to imagine
This had somehow all been planned
and the plan was matchless.
```

It will be obvious what seemed to me okay from the first draft and what did not. The basic structure seemed right: the first and last lines seemed right. I was specially pleased with 'matchless' because it echoes that mediaeval carol, 'I sing of a mayden who is makeles.' I had not heard it for a long time but I'm sure it was a shaping force behind the poem. At school I learned the Britten setting, and I can still sing it. I like vigorous, colloquial language, but 'stuck out' seemed clumsy, so I substituted 'thrust'. The main problem was describing the hand and what happened when I touched it. Should I talk about the hand or the fingers? I couldn't talk directly about the baby's fingers, because then I'd have a repetition when I spoke about 'her' finger. 'Wands' is a pretty feeble metaphor. I feel I want to do something more with the idea of the swimmers. Supposing I make each finger a swimmer? Is it too 'Martian'? I have always thought of fingers as miniature people, ao I'm not simply copying a manner. Let's try . . .

```
It was the crying hand
Thrust from the shawl, a sharp-petalled
Celandine in cold March grass:

It was the five little swimmers,
Sea-wearied, bent at the waist,
Waxed still in each hair-fine crease:

It was the sealed fortress
They built round her terrified finger
As the crying shivered into stillness

That made her think that the seeming
Shambles of it all was planned
And that the plan was matchless.
```

❖

As usual, I made changes as I typed: 'fully-opened' became 'sharp-petalled', and I added some descriptive detail about the finger-swimmers. A new idea came into the third stanza – that of the child somehow comforting and protecting the mother. I finally lost that: a pity, but in such a short, lyric form there is only room for so many ideas. I tried 'wall' instead of 'sealed fortress', then pencilled in 'strong-hold' but crossed it out.

```
It was the crying hand
Thrust from the shawl, a sharp-petalled
Celandine in cold March grass:

It was the five little swimmers,
Sea-wearied, bent at the waist,
Still waxed in each wrinkle and seam:

It was the stronghold they closed
Round her probing finger, the way
The crying shivered into stillness,

That made her think that the teeming
Shambles of it all was planned,
And the plan was matchless.
```

This was the version I considered finished enough to submit: it is the version framed and printed in the Birthright Exhibition catalogue. As soon as I saw it in print my eye flew to the repetition of 'Still' (1.6) and 'stillness' (1.9). Damn and blast! The more I look at it and say it to myself the uglier it becomes. I can't just get rid of that first 'still', not only because it fixes the swimmers in time, i.e. they've now finished swimming but only just, but because if I do I've got a horrid repetition of Ws ('waist' and 'waxed'). The other obvious device, to change 'stillness' to 'silence', also offends my ear: anyway, 'stillness' in the context has a much richer meaning than 'silence'. At the moment the problem seems insurmountable and it might even be better to leave it unsolved.

There are other worries. If the celandine is taken literally as a metaphor for the baby's hand it's clearly not right. What I meant to convey was suddenness: the celandine is always the first flower I see after winter, and the sight of it, so clean and bright on some ghastly grey March day, always moves me. I can't help if this sounds pseudo-Wordsworth. It's what I genuinely feel. I wonder if I should change 'sharp-petalled' to 'astonishing' or even 'sudden'. 'As sudden/as a celandine in cold March grass?' 'Abrupt' is better. But it doesn't convey the thrill, or the 'thereness' of the flower. I want to see the flower as well as the hand, but separate. I want the feel of utter newness, that is what they have in common.

The 'Martian' flavour of the 'swimmers' stanza still worries me, but I refuse to be intimidated by categories. I shall let it stand.

On the whole I like the poem. I like its sound, and the faint bits of rhyme ('hand' and 'planned', for example. Those words are far apart but I still think the echo can be heard. 'Distant rhyming' is something I'd like to explore further). I feel a strong emotion in the poem, I am moved by it. I think I've avoided sentimentality. I've certainly managed to avoid rhetoric, something I find very difficult when strong feelings are involved. My most deeply-felt poems always sound my most fake. I feel it's a very English poem. I just hope that scepticism comes through sufficiently. (A very English wish, that!)

It was the crying hand
Thrust from the shawl, unannounced
Celandine in cold March grass:

It was the five little swimmers,
Waxed in each wrinkle and seam,
Bent at waist, sea-wearied.

It was the stronghold they closed
Round her probing finger, the way
The crying shivered into stillness.

That made her think that the teeming
Shambles of it all was planned,
And the plan was matchless.

'Unannounced' now worries me because although it's true – or
seems true – of the flower, it's not really true of the baby, which
has been announcing its advent for the last nine months. I'm
reasonably pleased with stanza two now, having got rid of the
'still' and indicating the time-factor by making the line-order more
logical as narrative.

On reappraisal, 'unannounced' seems okay: after all, it's the
baby's hand I'm referring to, not the whole baby! I miss the 'still'
(still), and prefer the previous arrangement of stanza two after
all, but I shan't change back, as the repetition ('still' and
'stillness') seems to me the greater of two evils.

I *still* feel I may re-work it! I went on being dissatisfied with
version 5, and feeling that 4 was better, provided I got rid of
'sharp-petalled' and the 'still/stillness' repeats. I decided to try it
with a simile instead of a full metaphor in the first verse and
deleting 'stillness'.

```
It was the crying hand
Thrust from the shawl, unannounced
As celandines in March grass.

It was the five little swimmers,
Sea-wearied, bent at the waist,
Still waxed in each wrinkle and seam.

It was the stronghold they closed
Round her probing finger, the way
The crying shivered, and ceased,

That made her think that the teeming
Shambles of it all was planned,
And the plan was matchless.
```

Is that it? God, I hope so!

About this poem

- What light did Carol Rumens' commentary cast on the poem?

- In what ways did social factors such as her audience and her own cultural background influence her composition?

- How has she been influenced by other writing?

About writing in general

- Why do writers write?

- Where do they get inspiration?

- What influences the writing process?

EXTENSION ACTIVITY

Recall a moment of intensity or insight from your own experience and develop a poem from initial notes to finished version. Keep the drafts as you go and when you have finished, write a commentary in which you explain the decisions, choices and revisions that you made.

All writers experience pressures beyond the technical demands of their writing. These pressures are different, depending on the class, gender and circumstances of the writer. They also change over time. For many centuries, it was difficult for women and working people to write at all. They lacked the education, encouragement and time.

Not all poets re-draft extensively. Visit the manuscript room at the British Museum in London to see the range of drafting styles employed by writers.

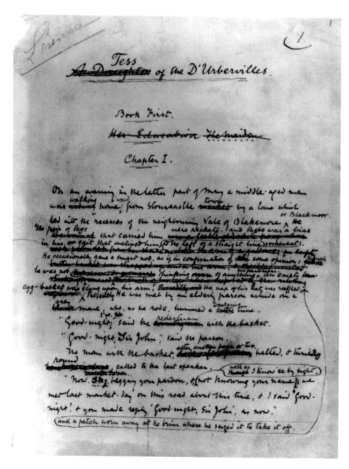

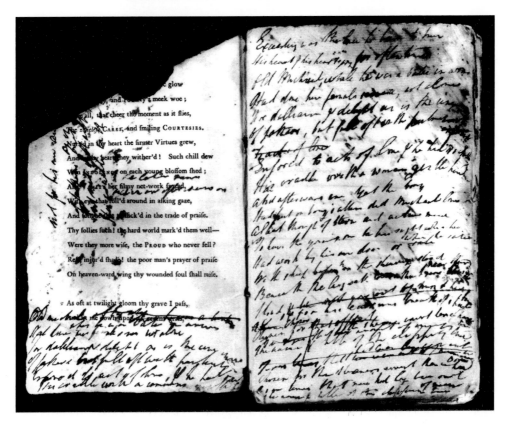

THE FORMAL ESSAY

AIMS

- to suggest ways of developing and organising ideas about literature
- to consider ways of expressing ideas for a more formal audience
- to introduce the conventions of the literary essay

ACTIVITY

- Read the following story once for your own pleasure and understanding, then share your reactions with other members of your group.

Chemistry

The pond in our park was circular, exposed, perhaps fifty yards across. When the wind blew, little waves travelled across it and slapped the paved edges, like a miniature sea. We would go there, Mother, Grandfather and I, to sail the motor-launch Grandfather and I made out of plywood, balsawood and varnished paper. We would go even in the winter – especially in the winter, because then we would have the pond to ourselves – when the leaves on the two willows turned yellow and dropped and the water froze your hands. Mother would sit on a wooden bench set back from the perimeter; I would prepare the boat for launching. Grandfather, in his black coat and grey scarf, would walk to the far side to receive it. For some reason it was always Grandfather, never I, who went to the far side. When he reached his station I would hear his 'Ready!' across the water. A puff of vapour would rise from his lips like the smoke from a muffled pistol. And I would release the launch. It worked by a battery. Its progress was laboured but its course steady. I would watch it head out to the middle while Mother watched behind me. As it moved it seemed that it followed an actual existing line between Grandfather, myself and Mother, as if Grandfather were pulling us towards him on some invisible cord, and that he had to do this to prove we were not beyond his reach. When the boat drew near him he would crouch on his haunches. His hands – which I knew were knotted, veiny and mottled from an accident in one of his chemical experiments – would reach out, grasp it and set it on its return.

The voyages were trouble-free. Grandfather improvised a wire grapnel on the end of the length of fishing line in case of shipwrecks or engine failure, but it was never used. Then one day – it must have been soon after Mother met Ralph – we watched the boat, on its first trip across the pond to Grandfather, suddenly become deeper, and deeper in the water. The motor cut. The launch wallowed, sank. Grandfather made several throws with his grapnel and pulled out clumps of green slime. I remember what he said to me, on this, the first loss in my life that I had witnessed. He said, very gravely: 'You must accept it – you can't get it back – it's the only way,' as if he were repeating something to himself. And I remember Mother's face as she got up from the bench to leave. It was very still and very white, as if she had seen something appalling.

It was some months after that that Ralph, who was now a regular guest at weekends, shouted over the table to Grandfather: 'Why don't you leave her alone?!'

I remember it because that same Saturday Grandfather recalled the wreck of my boat, and Ralph said to me, as if pouncing on something: 'How about me buying you a new one? How would you like that?' And I said, just to see his face go crestfallen and blank, 'No!', several times, fiercely. Then as we ate supper Ralph suddenly barked, as Grandfather was talking to Mother: 'Why don't you leave her alone?!'

Grandfather looked at him. 'Leave her alone? What do you know about being left alone?' Then he glanced from Ralph to Mother. And Ralph didn't answer, but his face went tight and his hands clenched on his knife and fork.

And all this was because Grandfather had said to Mother: 'You don't make curry any more, the way you did for Alec, the way Vera taught you.'

It was Grandfather's house we lived in – with Ralph as an ever more permanent lodger. Grandfather and Grandmother had lived in it almost since the day of their marriage. My grandfather had worked for a firm which manufactured gold- and silver-plated articles. My grandmother died suddenly when I was only four; and all I know is that I must have had her looks. My mother said so and so did my father; and Grandfather, without saying anything, would often gaze curiously into my face.

At that time Mother, Father and I lived in a new house some distance from Grandfather's. Grandfather took his wife's death very badly. He needed the company of his daughter and my father; but he refused to leave the house in which my grandmother had lived, and my parents refused to leave theirs. There was bitterness all round, which I scarcely appreciated. Grandfather remained alone in his house, which he ceased to maintain, spending more and more time in his garden shed which he had fitted out for his hobbies of model making and amateur chemistry.

The situation was resolved in a dreadful way: by my own father's death.

He was required now and then to fly to Dublin or Cork in the light aeroplane belonging to the company he worked for, which imported Irish goods. One day, in unexceptional weather conditions, the aircraft disappeared without trace into the Irish Sea. In a state which resembled a kind of trance – as if some outside force were all the time directing her – my Mother sold up our house, put away the money for our joint future, and moved in with Grandfather.

My father's death was a far less remote event than my grandmother's, but no more explicable. I was only seven. Mother said, amidst her adult grief: 'He has gone to where Grandma's gone.' I wondered how Grandmother could be at the bottom of the Irish Sea, and at the same time what Father was doing there. I wanted to know when he would return. Perhaps I knew, even as I asked this, that he never would, that my childish assumptions were only a way of allaying my own grief. But if I really believed Father was gone for ever – I was wrong.

Perhaps too I was endowed with my father's looks no less than my grandmother's. Because when my mother looked at me she would often break into uncontrollable tears and she would clasp me for long periods without letting go, as if afraid I might turn to air.

I don't know if Grandfather took a secret, vengeful delight in my father's death, or if he was capable of it. But fate had made him and his daughter quits and reconciled them in mutual grief.

Their situations were equivalent: she a widow and he a widower. And just as my mother could see in me a vestige of my father, so Grandfather could see in the two of us a vestige of my grandmother.

For about a year we lived quietly, calmly, even contentedly within the scope of this sad symmetry. We scarcely made any contact with the outside world. Grandfather still worked, though his retirement age had passed, and would not let Mother work. He kept Mother and me as he might have kept his own wife and son. Even when he did retire we lived quite comfortably on his pension, some savings and a widow's pension my mother got. Grandfather's health showed signs of weakening – he became rheumatic and sometimes short of breath – but he would still go out to the shed in the garden to conduct his chemical experiments, over which he hummed and chuckled gratefully to himself.

We forgot we were three generations. Grandfather bought Mother bracelets and ear-rings. Mother called me her 'little man'. We lived for each other – and for those two unfaded memories – and for a whole year, a whole harmonious year, we were really quite happy. Until that day in the park when my boat, setting out across the pond towards Grandfather, sank.

Sometimes when Grandfather provoked Ralph I thought Ralph would be quite capable of jumping to his feet, reaching across the table, seizing Grandfather by the throat and choking him. He was a big man, who ate heartily, and I was often afraid he might hit me. But Mother somehow kept him in check. Since Ralph's appearance she had grown neglectful of Grandfather. For example – as Grandfather had pointed out that evening – she would cook the things that Ralph liked (rich, thick stews, but not curry) and forget to produce the meals that Grandfather was fond of. But no matter how neglectful and even hurtful she might be to Grandfather herself, she wouldn't have forgiven someone else's hurting him. It would have been the end of her and Ralph. And no matter how much she might hurt Grandfather – to show her allegiance to Ralph – the truth was she really did want to stick by him. She still needed – she couldn't break free of it – that delicate equilibrium that she, he and I had constructed over the months.

I suppose the question was how far Ralph could tolerate not letting go with Grandfather so as to keep Mother, or how far Mother was prepared to turn against Grandfather so as not to lose Ralph. I remember keeping a sort of equation in my head: If Ralph hurts Grandfather it means I'm right – he doesn't really care about Mother at all; but if Mother is cruel to Grandfather (though she would only be cruel to him because she couldn't forsake him) it means she really loves Ralph.

But Ralph only went pale and rigid and stared at Grandfather without moving.

Grandfather picked at his stew. We had already finished ours. He deliberately ate slowly to provoke Ralph.

Then Ralph turned to Mother and said: 'For Christ's sake we're not waiting all night for him to finish!' Mother blinked and looked frightened. 'Get the pudding!'

You see, he liked his food.

Mother rose slowly and gathered our plates. She looked at me and said, 'Come and help.'

In the kitchen she put down the plates and leaned for several seconds, her back towards me, against the draining board. Then she turned. 'What am I going to do?' She gripped my shoulders. I remembered these were just the words she'd used once before, very soon after father's death, and then, her face had had the same quivery look of being about to spill over. She pulled me towards her. I had a feeling of being back in that old impregnable domain which Ralph had not yet penetrated. Through the window, half visible in the twilight, the evergreen shrubs which filled our garden were defying the onset of autumn. Only the cherry-laurel bushes were partly denuded – for some reason Grandfather had been picking their leaves. I didn't know what to do or say – I should have said something – but inside I was starting to form a plan.

Mother took her hands from me and straightened up. Her face was composed again. She took the apple-crumble from the oven. Burnt sugar and apple juice seethed for a moment on the edge of the dish. She handed me the bowl of custard. We strode, resolutely, back to the table. I thought: now we are going to face Ralph, now we are going to show our solidarity. Then she put down the crumble, began spooning out helpings and said to Grandfather, who was still tackling his stew: 'You're ruining our meal – do you want to take yours out to your shed?!'

Grandfather's shed was more than just a shed. Built in brick in one corner of the high walls surrounding the garden, it was large enough to accommodate a stove, a sink, an old armchair, as well as Grandfather's work-benches and apparatus, and to serve – as it was serving Grandfather more and more – as a miniature home.

I was always wary of entering it. It seemed to me, even before Ralph, even when Grandfather and I constructed the model launch, that it was somewhere where Grandfather went to be alone, undisturbed, to commune perhaps, in some obscure way, with my dead grandmother. But that evening I did not hesitate. I walked along the path by the ivy-clad garden wall. It seemed that his invitation, his loneliness were written in a form only I could read on the dark green door. And when I opened it he said: 'I thought you would come.'

I don't think Grandfather practised chemistry for any particular reason. He studied it from curiosity and for solace, as some people study the structure of cells under a microscope or watch the changing formation of clouds. In those weeks after Mother drove him out I learnt from Grandfather the fundamentals of chemistry.

I felt safe in his shed. The house where Ralph now lorded it, tucking into bigger and bigger meals, was a menacing place. The shed was another, a sealed-off world. It had a salty, mineral, unhuman smell. Grandfather's flasks, tubes and retort stands would be spread over his work-bench. His chemicals were acquired through connections in the metal-plating trade. The stove would be lit in the corner. Beside it would be his meal tray – for, to shame Mother, Grandfather had taken to eating his meals regularly in the shed. A single electric light bulb hung from a beam in the roof. A gas cylinder fed his bunsen. On one wall was a glass fronted cupboard in which he grew alum and copper sulphate crystals.

I would watch Grandfather's experiments. I would ask him to explain what he was doing and to name the contents of his various bottles.

And Grandfather wasn't the same person in his shed as he was in the house – sour and cantankerous. He was a weary, ailing man who winced now and then because of his rheumatism and spoke with quiet self-absorption.

'What are you making, Grandpa?'

'Not making – changing. Chemistry is the science of change. You don't make things in chemistry – you change them. Anything can change.'

He demonstrated the point by dissolving marble chips in nitric acid. I watched fascinated.

But he went on: 'Anything can change. Even gold can change.'

He poured a little of the nitric acid into a beaker, then took another jar of colourless liquid and added some of its contents to the nitric acid. He stirred the mixture with a glass rod and heated it gently. Some brown fumes came off.

'Hydrochloric acid and nitric acid. Neither would work by itself, but the mixture will.'

Lying on the bench was a pocket watch with a gold chain. I knew it had been given to Grandfather long ago by my grandmother. He unclipped the chain from the watch, then, leaning forward against the bench, he held it between two fingers over the beaker. The chain swung. He eyed me as if he were waiting for me to give some sign. Then he drew the chain away from the beaker.

'You'll have to take my word for it, eh?'

He picked up the watch and reattached it to the chain.

'My old job – gold-plating. We used to take real gold and change it. Then we'd take something that wasn't gold at all and cover it with this changed gold so it looked as if it was all gold – but it wasn't.'

He smiled bitterly.

'What are we going to do?'

'Grandpa?'

'People change too, don't they?'

He came close to me. I was barely ten. I looked at him without speaking.

'Don't they?'

He stared fixedly into my eyes, the way I remembered him doing after Grandmother's death.

'They change. But the elements don't change. Do you know what an element is? Gold's an element. We turned it from one form into another, but we didn't make any gold – or lose any.'

Then I had a strange sensation. It seemed to me that Grandfather's face before me was only a cross section from some infinite stick of rock, from which, at the right point, Mother's face and mine might also be cut. I thought: every face is like this. I had a sudden giddying feeling that there is no end to anything. I wanted to be told simple, precise facts.

'What's that, Grandpa?'

'Hydrochloric acid.'

'And that?'

'Green vitriol.'

'And that?' I pointed to another, unlabelled jar of clear liquid, which stood at the end of the bench, attached to a complex piece of apparatus.

'Laurel water. Prussic acid.' He smiled. 'Not for drinking.'

All the autumn was exceptionally cold. The evenings were chill and full of the rustlings of leaves. When I returned to the house from taking out Grandfather's meal tray (this had become my duty) I would observe Mother and Ralph in the living room through the open kitchen hatchway. They would drink a lot from the bottles of whisky and vodka which Ralph brought in and which at first Mother made a show of disapproving. The drink made Mother go soft and heavy and blurred and it made Ralph gain in authority. They would slump together on the sofa. One night I watched Ralph pull Mother towards him and hold her in his arms, his big lurching frame almost enveloping her, and Mother saw me, over Ralph's shoulder, watching from the hatchway. She looked trapped and helpless.

And that was the night that I got my chance – when I went to collect Grandfather's tray. When I entered the shed he was asleep in his chair, his plates, barely touched, on the tray at his feet. In his slumber – his hair dishevelled, mouth open – he looked like some torpid, captive animal that has lost even the will to eat. I had taken an empty spice jar from the kitchen, I took the glass bottle labelled HNO_3 and poured some of its contents, carefully, into the spice jar. Then I picked up Grandfather's tray, placed the spice jar beside the plates and carried the tray to the house.

I thought I would throw the acid in Ralph's face at breakfast. I didn't want to kill him. It would have been pointless to kill him – since death is a deceptive business. I wanted to spoil his face so Mother would no longer want him. I took the spice jar to my room and hid it in my bedside cupboard. In the morning I would smuggle it down in my trouser pocket. I would wait, pick my moment. Under the table I would remove the stopper. As Ralph gobbled down his eggs and fried bread . . .

I thought I would not be able to sleep. From my bedroom window I could see the dark square of the garden and a little patch of light cast from the window of Grandfather's shed. Often I could not sleep until I had seen that patch of light disappear and I knew that Grandfather had shuffled back to the house and slipped in, like a stray cat, the back door.

But I must have slept that night, for I do not remember seeing Grandfather's light go out or hearing his steps on the garden path.

That night Father came to my bedroom. I knew it was him. His hair and clothes were wet, his lips were caked with salt; seaweed hung from his shoulders. He came and stood by my bed. Where he trod, pools of water formed on the carpet and slowly oozed outwards. For a long time he looked at me. Then he said: 'It was her. She made a hole on the bottom of the boat, not big enough to notice, so it would sink – so you and Grandfather would watch it sink. The boat sank – like my plane.' He gestured

to his dripping clothes and encrusted lips. 'Don't you believe me?'
He held out a hand to me but I was afraid to take it. 'Don't you
believe me? Don't you believe me?' And as he repeated this he
walked slowly backwards towards the door, as if something were
pulling him, the pools of water at his feet drying instantly. And it
was only when he had disappeared that I managed to speak and
said: 'Yes. I believe you. I'll prove it.'

And then it was almost light and rain was dashing against the
window as if the house were plunging under water and a strange,
small voice was calling from the front of the house – but it wasn't
Father's voice. I got up, walked out onto the landing and peered
through the landing window. The voice was a voice on the radio
inside an ambulance which was parked with its doors open by the
pavement. The heavy rain and the tossing branches of a rowan
tree obscured my view, but I saw the two men in uniform
carrying out the stretcher with a blanket draped over it. Ralph
was with them. He was wearing his dressing gown and pyjamas
and slippers over bare feet, and he carried an umbrella. He fussed
around the ambulance men like an overseer directing the loading
of some vital piece of cargo. He called something to Mother who
must have been standing below, out of sight at the front door. I
ran back across the landing. I wanted to get the acid. But then
Mother came up the stairs. She was wearing her dressing gown.
She caught me in her arms. I smelt whisky. She said: 'Darling.
Please, I'll explain. Darling, darling.'

But she never did explain. All her life since then, I think, she
was been trying to explain, or to avoid explaining. She only said:
'Grandpa was old and ill, he wouldn't have lived much longer
anyway.' And there was the official verdict: suicide by swallowing
prussic acid. But all the other things that should have been
explained – or confessed – she never did explain.

And she wore, beneath everything, this look of relief, as if she
had recovered from an illness. Only a week after Grandfather's
funeral she went into Grandfather's bedroom and flung wide the
windows. It was a brilliant, crisp late-November day and the
leaves on the rowan tree were all gold. And she said: 'There –
isn't that lovely?'

The day of Grandfather's funeral had been such a day – hard,
dazzling, spangled with early frost and gold leaves. We stood at the
ceremony, Mother, Ralph and I, like a mock version of the trio –
Grandfather, Mother and I – who had once stood at my father's
memorial service. Mother did not cry. She had not cried at all, even
in the days before the funeral when the policemen and the officials

from the coroner's court came, writing down their statements, apologising for their intrusion and asking their questions.

They did not address their questions to me. Mother said: 'He's only ten, what can he know?' Though there were a thousand things I wanted to tell them – about how Mother banished Grandfather, about how suicide can be murder and how things don't end – which made me feel that I was somehow under suspicion. I took the jar of acid from my bedroom, went to the park and threw it in the pond.

And then after the funeral, after the policemen and officials had gone, Mother and Ralph began to clear out the house and to remove the things from the shed. They tidied the overgrown parts of the garden and clipped back the trees. Ralph wore an old sweater which was far too small for him and I recognised it as one of Father's. And Mother said: 'We're going to move to a new house soon – Ralph's buying it.'

I had nowhere to go. I went down to the park and stood by the pond. Dead willow leaves floated on it. Beneath its surface was a bottle of acid and the wreck of my launch. But though things change they aren't destroyed. It was there, by the pond, when dusk was gathering and it was almost time for the park gates to be locked, as I looked to the centre where my launch sank, then up again to the far side, that I saw him. He was standing on his black overcoat and his grey scarf. The air was very cold and little waves were running across the water. He was smiling, and I knew: the laugh was still travelling over to him, unstoppable, unsinkable, along that invisible line. And his hands, his acid-marked hands, would reach out to receive it.

As you work through this unit, you will be focusing on different aspects of this story's composition. Eventually you will organise an essay plan around one of these ideas and write it up.

Exploring the text

- Read the story again, paying special attention to how the story is told.

As you read, keep track of
- shifts in time
- what we learn about the narrator
- the voice and style of the telling

- Before you start, consider which forms of recording will be most useful, for example:

- shifts in time (timeline? list? notes in the margin? diagram?)
- narrator (underlining? star chart? list? quotations?)
- telling (highlighting? list of impressions? sample quotations?)

- When you have finished reading and annotating, work in a group to create a large diagram to represent the relationships in this story.
  Then spend five or ten minutes reflecting on the significance of chemistry in the story and write down your ideas.

- Pool your ideas with other people's before moving on.

Organising ideas

In this section, you are going to gather ideas for an essay and put them in order. Here is an example of a brainstorm for an essay about the way the story is told.

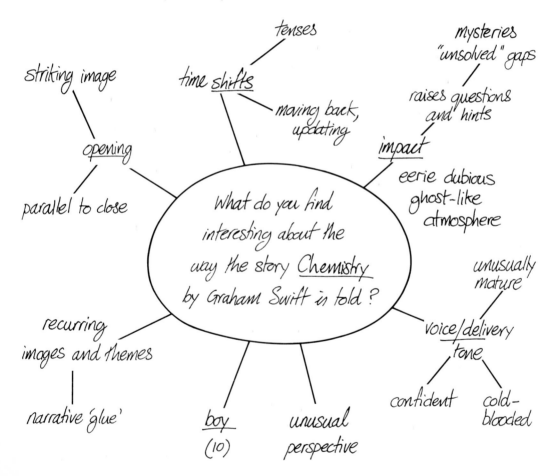

A star chart is a good strategy for gathering together a range of ideas about a subject. It would not be so useful if you had been asked to make a comparison. In that case, two columns might have served better. An essay title which asks you to trace developments through a text could be planned using a flow diagram.

The star chart does not show which points are most important, so they have to be put into a sequence which reflects their importance and which allows you to lead easily from one point to the next. For example:

1 The opening of the story
2 Facts about the boy
3 Unusual perspective
4 Voice
5 Time shifts
6 Recurring images
7 Overview/conclusion

- You may find it useful to consider a plan for a further essay title about the relationship between the narrator and his family. The main branches of the diagram have been prepared, but you can add more if you wish. Use a large sheet of paper to cluster ideas around these key areas, incorporating short quotations you could use in an essay.

father dead

circumstances

relationship with others

Mother

How does Graham Swift present the relationships between the boy and his family in the short story *Chemistry?*

Perspective, through boy's eyes

family "chemistry"

- Now decide on the sequence of your points for an essay.

- Here is a title for you to plan by first brainstorming ideas and then putting them into a sequence. Consider in advance where the emphasis of the title lies, and what strategies you will use to gather ideas.

Describe the character of the mother in Graham Swift's story *Chemistry* and discuss the role she plays in the story.

Expressing ideas

Many students find the opening the most daunting part of an essay, although there is no reason why you should start a first draft by writing the introduction. Even in an examination it is possible to leave a space to return to later.

- Below are six examples of students' introductions to the above essay. Read them through and review their strengths and weaknesses.

'The Grandfather is clearly a proud man with strong principles and values. He cared for his daughter and grandson and is looking after them. His one hobby was chemistry which had left him with many scars on his hands'

'As the story starts the young boy is already trying to explain what has already happened to his mother. He tries to explain that his mother has been through two deaths, the first of her mother then of her husband. From the very beginning the love between mother and son is showed openly in many ways. Such as "when my mother looked at me she would often break down into uncontrollable tears."

'To understand and explain the role the mother plays in the story we must first look at her background'.

'The relationships in this story are viewed through the eyes of a ten-year-old boy. His narrative focuses on events which happened in the first ten years of his life, presenting scenes through time-shifts. The writer begins and concludes his story at the pond in the park and this circular dimension runs consistently through the piece'.

'In this essay I am going to write about the interesting way the short story "Chemistry" by Graham Swift is told. I am going to look at many aspects of the story but probably the most significant of these is the title and themes of the whole story "Chemistry" and the way it influences many different changes through the story.'

'Graham Swift presents the relationships in "Chemistry" in a number of different ways depending on the circumstances, the boy's relationships with others, the perspective through the boy's eyes and the family "chemistry".'

- Now write your own introduction and share it. If necessary, revise it in the light of the comments of the group.
- List some of the qualities of a good opening to this type of essay.
- Imagine you are writing the essay about the way the story is told, and you are going to write the paragraph about the distinctive features of the narrator's voice. Here are some of your notes:

Voice
— very adult, mature sounding

— formal, distant, almost cold-blooded

— controlled, literary style

You have picked out the following quotes which might be useful:

'My father's death was a far less remote event than my grandmother's but no more explicable'
'But fate had made him and his daughter quits and reconciled them in mutual grief'
'For about a year we lived quietly, calmly, even contentedly within the scope of this sad symmetry'

- Using these ideas and any of your own, write the opening sentences of the paragraph about the narrator's voice, incorporating appropriate quotation.
- Share your sentences and consider the various ways of incorporating quotation. One of the advantages of using brief snatches of text is that you can fit them into your own sentences.
- Choose one of the essay titles and write an essay which is about four sides of A4 paper in length.

Conventions of the literature essay

Imagine you are writing for an interested reader who knows the texts and likes to see ideas developed and explained.

Write in Standard English, that is, using formal language which avoids slang. Be precise but don't be pompous.

Personal opinions are welcome. Explain them and provide evidence.

Incorporate quotation only if it supports an argument and justifies and develops your point. Acknowledge quotation by using quotation marks. Several short quotations are more effective than one long one. If you do use a substantial quotation, however, leave space all around it so it is easy to locate in the text.

CONVENTIONS OF THE LITERATURE ESSAY

Imagine you are writing for an interested reader who knows the texts and likes to see ideas developed and explained.

Write in standard English, using formal language which avoids using slang. Be precise but don't be pompous.

Personal opinions are welcome. Explain them and provide evidence.

Incorporate quotation only if it supports an argument and justifies and develops your point. Acknowledge quotation by using quotation marks. Several short quotations are more effective than one long one. If you do use a substantial quotation, however, leave space around all around it so it is easy to locate in the text.

where the pace of the narrative starts to change:

"...

....

....

.... "

It is at this point that the reader...

There are many ways to write about literature, but one of the most common formats at advanced level is the essay in which you are required to discuss literary ideas in a formal way. This is particularly true in examinations. It is not necessarily the best way to give a written response to texts. Creative responses such as your own writing, an imitation of the text's style, or taking the perspective of a character can prove very illuminating.

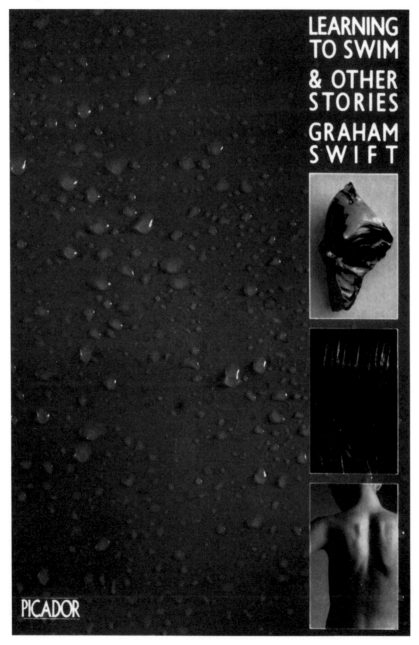

LEARNING TO SWIM & OTHER STORIES
GRAHAM SWIFT

PICADOR